THE BLUE FAIRY BOOK

Edited by Andrew Lang

Teacher Guide

David M. Wright

MEMORIA PRESS
www.MemoriaPress.com

THE BLUE FAIRY BOOK
Edited by Andrew Lang

TEACHER GUIDE
David M. Wright

ISBN 978-1-61538-388-7

Cover illustration by Arthur Rackham

Contents

Teaching Guidelines **4**

Prince Hyacinth and the Dear Little Princess 6
Cinderella, or the Little Glass Slipper 8
Beauty and the Beast 10
Why the Sea is Salt 12
Felicia and the Pot of Pinks 14
Snow-White and Rose-Red 16
Toads and Diamonds 18
The Princess on the Glass Hill 20
Prince Darling 22
Hansel and Grettel 24
Additional Space for Composition (Enrichment) Exercises 26

Discussion Question Answers **29**

Quizzes & Tests **35**
Quiz 1 36
Quiz 2 38
Quiz 3 40
Quiz 4 42
Final Exam 44
Quiz 1 Answer Key 50
Quiz 2 Answer Key 52
Quiz 3 Answer Key 54
Quiz 4 Answer Key 56
Final Exam Answer Key 58

PREPARING TO READ:

REVIEW

- Orally review any previous vocabulary.
- If need be, review fairy tales read thus far.
- Periodically review the concepts of character, setting, plot, and theme.

STUDY GUIDE PREVIEW

- Reading Notes:
  - Read aloud together.
  - This section gives the students key characters, places, vocabulary, and literary terms that are relevant to the particular fairy tale.
- Vocabulary:
  - Have students attempt to determine the right word from the word from the Definitions Bank. It is also helpful to read the vocabulary words aloud together so that students will recognize the words when they come across them in their reading.
- Comprehension Questions:
  - At your discretion, read through these questions (or some) with students to encourage purposeful reading.

READING:

- Students should read the fairy tale (or a section of the fairy tale) independently. The other good option is to have students read sections of the fairy tale aloud.
- For younger students, you can alternate between teacher-read and student-read passages. Model good reading skills. Encourage students to read expressively and smoothly. The teacher may occasionally take oral reading grades.
- While reading, mark each vocabulary word as you come across it.
- Have students take note in their study guide margin of the particular pages where a Comprehension Question is answered.

AFTER READING:

VOCABULARY

- Look at each word within the context that it is used by reading a sentence or two before and after the word. Discuss the definition given in the Definitions Bank. It can also be helpful to discuss some additional synonyms for the word.
- Record the word's meaning in the students' study guides, writing it exactly as it appears in the Definitions Bank. (If possible, use students' knowledge of Latin and other vocabulary in your discussion of the definitions.)

COMPREHENSION QUESTIONS

- Older students can answer these questions independently, but younger students (2nd-4th) need to answer the questions orally, then form a good sentence, and then write it down, using correct punctuation, capitalization, and spelling. (For younger students, you may want to write the sentence down after forming it orally, and then let students copy it perfectly.)
- It is not necessary to write the answer to every question. Some may be better answered orally.
- Answering questions and composing answers is a valuable learning activity. Questions require students to think; writing a concise answer is a good composition exercise.

QUOTATIONS AND DISCUSSION QUESTIONS

- Use the Quotations and Discussion Questions sections of each lesson as a guide to your oral discussion of the key concepts in the fairy tale that may not be covered in the Comprehension Questions.
- These Quotations and Discussion Questions help take the students' understanding of the fairy tale to a higher level than what is covered in the Vocabulary and Comprehension Questions. Use this time as an opportunity to introduce complexity in their thinking. Here you can introduce concepts that the students may not fully understand yet, but would be beneficial for them to begin thinking about.
- A key to the Discussion Questions is in the back of the Teacher Guide. The answers are short; you should elaborate on the answers in your discussion.

ENRICHMENT

- The Enrichment activities include composition, copywork, dictation, research, drawing, poetry, literary terms, and more.
- This section has a variety of activities in it, but the most valuable activity is composition. Your students should complete at least one composition assignment each week. Proof students' work and have students copy composition until grammatically perfect. Insist on clear, concise writing. For younger students, start with 2-3 sentences, and do the assignment together. The students can form good sentences orally as you write them down, and then the students copy them.
- You may find that there is not enough room for composition in the Enrichment section. Two additional lined pages are provided in the back of the study guide for additional space.
- These Enrichment activities can be completed as time and interest allow. Do not feel you need to complete all of these activities. Choose the ones that you feel are the best use of your students' time.

UNIT REVIEW AND TESTS

- There is a quiz covering every two fairy tales.
- On the weeks that have these quizzes, you may want to review early in the week, and then drill it orally a couple of times before giving the quiz at the end of the week.
- The final exam is longer and covers the last two fairy tales.

"You shall have a son, who will never be happy until he finds out that his nose is too long ..."

Reading Notes

enchantment a spell or some kind of magic

Roman nose a prominent or slightly curved nose

Prince Hyacinth the son of the King and Princess; He was given a long nose from the enchanter because his father, the King, broke the enchantment of his mother, the Princess.

Vocabulary

Definitions Bank

not able to be comforted

the act of comparing things to see how they are alike or different

terrible; horrible

wonderful; beautiful

1. The Queen was **inconsolable** when she saw this great nose not able to be comforted
2. they told him all sorts of **dreadful** stories terrible; horrible
3. But, do what they would, they were nothing by **comparison** the act of comparing things to see how they are alike or different
4. The Prince made him a **splendid** present wonderful; beautiful

Comprehension Questions

1. In the beginning of the story, what must the King do to break the enchantment of the Princess whom he loves? Does he succeed? He must tread on the Princess's cat's tail. Yes, he is able to step on the tail and break the enchantment.
2. Who appears "as suddenly as a flash of lightning" and snatches the Dear Little Princess away just as Prince Hyacinth is about to kiss her hand? the enchanter
3. What important person does Prince Hyacinth meet on his journey to find the Dear Little Princess? He meets the old woman,who is really a fairy.

4. Why does she turn out to be so important? Because she begins, through several comments, to bring the truth to Hyacinth that his nose is unusually long.

5. What happens when Prince Hyacinth says, "Well, it must be admitted that my nose *is* too long!"? The crystal prison flies into a thousand pieces, and there is the old Fairy and the Dear Little Princess. And now Prince Hyacinth's nose is the right size!

Quotations

"Now, say if you are not very much obliged to me. Much good it was for me to talk to you about your nose! You would never have found out how extraordinary it was if it hadn't hindered you from doing what you wanted to. You see how self-love keeps us from knowing our own defects of mind and body. Our reason tries in vain to show them to us; we refuse to see them till we find them in the way of our interests."

1. Who said this? the old Fairy

Discussion Questions

1. For most of the story, Prince Hyacinth thought his nose was the right size, and everyone else's nose was too small. Whom do you think is most to blame for Prince Hyacinth's faulty view of his nose?
2. Why do you suppose the Dear Little Princess was snatched away just as Prince Hyacinth was about to kiss her hand?

Enrichment

1. From the quotation above, can you find the two sentences that teach an important life lesson? With good penmanship, copy the two sentences below.
"You see how self-love keeps us from knowing our own defects of mind and body. Our reason tries in vain to show them to us; we refuse to see them till we find them in the way of our interests."

"... putting the slipper to her foot, he found it went on very easily, and fitted her as if it had been made of wax."

Reading Notes

cinder a partially burned piece of coal or wood

symbol something that stands for something else; an object that has a range of meaning or significance beyond itself

godmother a woman who serves as a sponsor and protector of a child, usually at a baptism

Vocabulary

Definitions Bank

good manners; politeness

surprise; amazement

twisted or turned; not straight

unpleasant; hateful

1. they made her own daughters appear the more **odious** unpleasant; hateful
2. Anyone but Cinderella would have dressed their heads **awry** twisted or turned; not straight
3. She went and sat down by her sisters, showing them a thousand **civilities** good manners; politeness
4. The **astonishment** her two sisters were in surprise; amazement

Comprehension Questions

1. Why could Cinderella's stepmother not "bear the good qualities of this pretty girl"? Because Cinderella's good qualities made her own daughters appear all the more odious.
2. List three jobs that Cinderella's stepmother demanded she do. scour the dishes and tables; scrub madam's and her daughters' chambers; iron the sisters' linens and plait their ruffles
3. As the two sisters were preparing for the ball, "anyone but Cinderella would have dressed their heads awry, but Cinderella dressed them perfectly well." Why do you think Cinderella still dressed them neatly? What does this reveal about her? Cinderella still dressed them neatly because she has excellent, virtuous character. It reveals how good and pure Cinderella is.

4. After Cinderella's fairy godmother changes her clothes into the most beautfiul attire, what specific command does she give her? And what will happen if Cinderella breaks the command? The command is to not stay one moment after midnight. If she does, all of her coach, horses, coachmen, footmen, and clothes will become just as they were before.

5. How does Cinderella treat her sisters when it is discovered that the glass slipper fits her and she is the beautiful lady? She forgives them with all of her heart. She even offers her sisters lodging in the palace.

Quotations

"There came thither the finest princess, the most beautiful ever was seen with mortal eyes; she showed us a thousand civilities, and gave us oranges and citrons."

1. Who said this? one of the sisters

Discussion Questions

1. Why do you think Cinderella's sisters treated her so terribly? Was it just because Cinderella was their stepsister, or something more?
2. Of what significance is the glass slipper? Could the glass slipper be a symbol for something more important or greater?

Enrichment

1. Draw a picture of an object from your childhood that means much more to you than simply the material that the object is made of. In other words, draw a picture of an object that is very special to you!

"See if any one of them is courageous enough, and loves you well enough to come and save your life."

Reading Notes

setting — the time and place of a story

Central Idea — not necessarily the most important thing that happens in a story, but the most important *idea* in the story

lament — to express regret or disappointment

Vocabulary

Definitions Bank

deserted; empty

wasteful and careless spending

extreme tiredness; exhaustion

wise; sensible

1. All that he had left was a little house in a **desolate** place deserted; empty
2. even attributed their misfortunes to their own **extravagance** wasteful and careless spending
3. but their father, who was more **prudent**, begged them to wait a little wise; sensible
4. he was almost exhausted with cold and **fatigue** extreme tiredness; exhaustion

Comprehension Questions

1. What is the first major misfortune that happens to the merchant and his twelve children?
   Their house catches fire and burns to the ground, along with all of their splendid furniture, books, pictures, gold, silver, and precious goods. The father also lost every ship he owned on the sea.
2. What two things does Beauty wish for from her father when he goes on a journey to retrieve his lost ship?
   First she wishes only for her father to come home safely. Then, upon her father's insistence, she asks for a rose.
3. When the merchant returns home after attempting to retrieve the goods from his ship, what element of **setting** becomes a dangerous obstacle to him? The weather (deep snow and bitter frost) becomes a dangerous obstacle. It also became night.

4. What does the Beast demand of the merchant? The Beast demands that he send one of his daughters who will willingly come in his place in order to save him.

5. What are some of the physical objects that Beauty sees in the castle to indicate that her dreams contain real and true messages? The bracelet, hanging from the chandelier, contains a portrait of the Prince from her dream. She also sees portraits of the Prince on the wall, which even seem to wink at her.

6. Why does Beauty feel she must return to the Beast after two months? Answers will vary. First, she promised the Beast. Second, the Beast says he will die if she does not return, and she also has a sad dream of the Beast dying. And third, perhaps it is because she has fallen in love with the Beast and has begun to distrust appearances!

Quotations

"… and in making me happy you will find your own happiness. Be as true-hearted …"

1. Who said this? the prince in Beauty's dream

Discussion Questions

1. What sets Beauty apart from her sisters?
2. What do you think is the most important idea in the story? Could Beauty's dream contain the most important idea?

Enrichment

1. Copy a passage (a sentence or two) that you feel contains the Central Idea, the most important idea in the story.
   Answers will vary: "The only thing that at all disturbed her was to be constantly told to distrust appearances, to let her heart guide her, and not her eyes."
   Or: "Only be grateful," he answered, "and do not trust too much to your eyes."
   Or: "Dear Beauty, try not to regret all you have left behind you, for you are destined to a better fate. Only do not let yourself be deceived by appearances."

"But you must not sell it unless you can get the hand-mill which stands behind the door for it. When you come out again I will teach you how to stop the hand-mill, which is useful for almost everything."

Reading Notes

wise old man — a wise fatherly figure who often appears as a grandfather, professor, or wizard, etc.; usually moral, kind, and wise, and provides help and guidance

Dead Man's Hall — a place where the souls of those who have not been very good go after death

herring — a silvery fish abundant in coastal waters that is a common food in many parts of the world

pottage — a thick soup or stew

Vocabulary

Definitions Bank

bickered and argued over the price
required; compelled
dangerous; unsafe
harm or trouble

1. and **haggled** and bargained with the man bickered and argued over the price
2. he cried as he went by them as if **mischief** were at his heels harm or trouble
3. But the brother would not take it until the other paid him three hundred dollars, and that he was **obliged** to do. required; compelled
4. having to sail far away over the **perilous** sea for freights of salt dangerous; unsafe

Comprehension Questions

1. When the poor man gets home with the hand-mill, what is the first thing he asks it to grind?
   Christmas Eve supper
2. *"'Bless me!' said the old woman as one thing after another appeared; and she wanted to know where her husband had got the mill from, but he would not tell her that."*

   Why do you think the poor man would not tell his wife where he got the hand-mill when she asked him?
   He feels guilty, uncomfortable, or nervous about where the hand-mill came from. (I should think he would—It's a hand-mill from hell! ☺)

3. What is the rich brother's reaction to the poor brother's banquet feast that he throws for all his friends? "He was both vexed and angry, for he grudged everything his brother had."

4. What did the women and the mowers meet on their way home for dinner? herrings, pottage, and bread pouring down the hill

5. Why does the skipper want the hand-mill so desperately? With the hand-mill, he could get off having to sail far away over the perilous sea for freights of salt.

6. What happened to the skipper? And why is the sea salty? The skipper could not turn off the hand-mill, so it kept grinding salt and sank his ship. It continues to grind salt at the bottom of the sea.

Quotations

"Would to heaven that each of you had a hundred stomachs! Take care that you are not drowned in the pottage!"

1. Who said this? the rich brother

Discussion Questions

1. Did the poor brother *intentionally* not tell his rich brother how to stop the mill? Do you agree with the poor brother?

Enrichment

1. Draw a picture of the hand-mill grinding salt at the bottom of the sea. Use colored pencils so that your picture will have detail and color.

"But you have a heart," said the Queen. "What should you say if anybody wanted to steal that?"

Reading Notes

Queen of the Woods a magic Queen

stately dignified; majestic

zephyrs West winds

Vocabulary

Definitions Bank

extreme edge

made a low, continuing sound

painfully; emotionally

to beg; to ask for earnestly

1. but she cried more **bitterly** than ever painfully; emotionally
2. When she reached it she sat down upon the **brink** to rest extreme edge
3. and the falling water **murmured** the softest music made a low, continuing sound
4. Don't keep me in suspense, I **entreat** you; say that you will marry me. to beg; to ask for earnestly

Comprehension Questions

1. What is the difference between Felicia and her brother, Bruno? Felicia is gentle; Bruno is cruel.
2. What magical thing does the Queen do to Felicia's pitcher and the water? She turns the pitcher to gold with sparkling diamonds; the water she makes fragrant with the smell of roses.
3. What does Felicia offer the Queen instead of the pot of pinks? What does this say about her character? She offers the Queen her ring. It is the only possession of value that Felicia has left, so it reveals her great generosity, humility, and kindness.
4. What did Felicia's mother, the Queen, do to escape from the tower with Felicia? And then where did she go, and what did she do with Felicia? She escaped with Felicia from the tower window by means of a rope ladder. She wandered about till she was half dead with cold and fatigue. She left Felicia in the charge of her nurse.

5. What three unusual things speak to Felicia, which, after the third, cause her to become pale and faint?
a cabbage, a hen, and a pink

6. Whom does Felicia turn out to be? And whom does she marry? She turns out to be a princess.
She marries the Queen of the Woods' son, a prince who had been turned into a pink.

Quotations

"Don't imagine that you are the daughter of the poor labourer who brought you up; your mother was a queen who had six girls already, and the King threatened that unless she had a son …"

1. Who said this? the hen

Discussion Questions

1. Does Felicia show compassion to Bruno? Do you think she should have?
2. Felicia says, "Ah! madam … I am so happy that I should like everybody else to be happy too." Reflect on her words here. What virtues do they reveal?

Enrichment

1. *"'Ah! madam,' she answered simply, 'if I have your friendship I shall do very well.'"*
When Felicia says this to the Queen of the Woods, she reveals her kindness and humility. She is willing to give up her last possession for the Queen's friendship. Write a paragraph about a good friend who is special to you. Be sure to include descriptive details, and perhaps even a quote of something your friend said (include quotation marks).

"Couldn't you have treated me more carefully? You have torn my thin little coat all to shreds ...!"

Reading Notes

dwarfs mythological beings that dwell in mountains and in the earth; they are often described as short and ugly

trudge to walk slowly and laboriously

perceive to become aware of; to recognize

Vocabulary

Definitions Bank

being unthankful or ungrateful

careful; hardworking

a cliff or steep ledge

trusting; confidential

1. they were the sweetest and best children in the world, always **diligent** and always cheerful careful; hardworking
2. they came up to them in the most **confiding** manner trusting; confidential
3. they had slept quite close to a **precipice** a cliff or steep ledge
4. The girls were accustomed to his **ingratitude** being unthankful or ungrateful

Comprehension Questions

1. Who do you think the beautiful child in a shining white robe is? And why do you think the child appears there when the children wake up? The passage suggests that it is a guardian angel who appears there to protect the children from falling off the precipice.
2. Describe how each person and creature reacts when the bear pokes his head through the door. Rose-Red screams aloud and springs back; the lamb bleats; the dove flaps its wings; Snow-White runs and hides behind her mother.
3. From whom does the bear want to protect his treasure? Describe the creature. The bear wants to protect his treasure from the wicked dwarfs. The creature has a beard a yard long and fiery red eyes. He is mean and surly, screaming, "What are you standing there for? Can't you come and help me?"

4. How do the girls continually free the wicked creature? They cut part of his beard each time.

5. After the children free the dwarf, what does he eagerly reach for each time? a sack of gold, a sack of pearls, and a sack of precious stones

6. What connection does the dwarf have with the bear? The bear is really the king's son. He was doomed by the dwarf, who stole his treasure, to roam about the woods as a wild bear until the dwarf's death set him free.

Quotations

"Dear Mr. Bear, spare me! I'll give you all my treasure. Look at those beautiful precious stones lying there."

1. Who said this? The dwarf

Discussion Questions

1. Why do you think the mother carries the red and white rose trees with her wherever she goes?
2. What vice or character flaw does the dwarf have that makes him so rotten?

Enrichment

1. Draw a picture of the red and white rose trees. In the trunk of the trees, or in one or two of the branches, draw a carving of the girls' names, Snow-White and Rose-Red.

"Am I come hither," said the proud, saucy one, "to serve you with water, pray? I suppose the silver tankard was brought purely for your ladyship, was it?"

Reading Notes

courtesy good manners; civility; respect

infinite limitless or endless

Vocabulary

Definitions Bank

a strong dislike

politeness; courtesy

showed excessive fondness or love

complaining; muttering

1. this mother even **doted** on her eldest daughter showed excessive fondness or love
2. and at the same time had a horrible **aversion** for the youngest a strong dislike
3. to see how far the **civility** and good manners of this pretty girl would go politeness; courtesy
4. So away she went, but **grumbling** all the way complaining; muttering

Comprehension Questions

1. What are the two character traits of the mother and eldest daughter mentioned in the beginning of the story? They are disagreeable and proud.
2. How does the youngest daughter respond to the old woman who asks her for a drink? Quote what the daughter says (use quotation marks). She responds with kindness and love. "Oh! ay, with all my heart, Goody."
3. Why does the Fairy take the form of an old country woman? "to see how far the civility and good manners of this pretty girl would go"
4. What first comes out of the younger daughter's mouth? two roses, two pearls, and two diamonds
5. How does the Fairy appear to the eldest daughter, Fanny? How does Fanny respond to her? She appears as a gloriously dressed princess. The daughter treats her rudely.

6. What comes out of Fanny's mouth when she returns? Whom does her mother blame for this? two vipers and two toads; She blames the younger sister.

7. What happens to the younger daughter at the end? The King's son finds her on his return from hunting. She tells him her whole story; he falls in love with her and marries her.

Quotations

"Wouldst not thou be glad, my dear, to have the same gift given thee? Thou hast nothing else to do but go and draw water out of the fountain, and when a certain poor woman asks you to let her drink, to give it to her very civilly."

1. Who said this? The mother (to Fanny)

2. Why did she say this? Because she saw the roses, pearls, and diamonds come out of the younger daughter's mouth, and she wanted such a fortune to be given to Fanny and herself.

Discussion Questions

1. Do you think that what comes out of the daughters' mouths is symbolic?
2. Discuss the **title** of the fairy tale. Does it capture what is most important in the tale?

Enrichment

1. Consider what you have learned from this story. Write out some of the ways that we can treat others better. Perhaps people are not always how they appear?

"Then everything became still as death again."

Reading Notes

St. John's Eve The evening of June 23 is the eve of celebration before the feast day of St. John the Baptist, June 24.

simile a comparison of two different things by using *like*, *as*, or *than* (see quote above)

accoutrements equipment; items worn for a particular activity

Vocabulary

Definitions Bank

distant; remote   bet; gamble   healthy growth   sparkled; glittered; shined

1. when the grass was in the height of its **vigor** healthy growth
2. when the youth heard it he was terrified, and went off, running as if for a **wager** bet; gamble
3. when evening drew near rambled away to the **outlying** field distant; remote
4. all were so bright that they shone and **glistened** sparkled; glittered; shined

Comprehension Questions

1. *"... and the lad jumped up and took to his heels as fast as he could, and never even looked back, and the barn remained empty that year just as it had been for the last two."*

   Why did the barn remain empty that year just as it had been for the last two? There has been very little hay in the barn for the last couple years because every St. John's Eve, the grass of the fields is eaten clean up during the night.

2. What happens to the first two brothers when they attempt to spend the night in the barn? They hear a great rumbling, then there is an earthquake. They become terrified and run back home.

3. What does Cinderlad see when he survives the night in the barn? Describe in detail. He sees a big, fat, fine horse eating the grass. It has a saddle and a bridle on it, and also a complete suit of armor for a knight. Everything is copper, bright and shining.

4. What does Cinderlad do each time he sees the horse on St. John's Eve? He pulls out his steel for striking fire, throws it over the horse to tame it, mounts the horse, and rides it to the place where he keeps the others.

5. Describe the competition that the King sets up in order to offer his daughter's hand in marriage. He will only give his daughter (and half his kingdom) to the person who can ride to the top of the glass hill and take the three gold apples from her lap.

6. Each time the knight appears, his saddle and armor are of a different metal. What are the three metals? copper, silver, and gold

7. Refer to the definition of **simile** in the Reading Notes and to the quote at the top of page 20. Now, find two **similes** in the story and write them here. Here are some, but probably not all: "running as if for a wager"; "suddenly grew as still as death"; "stood as still as if it had been nailed to the field"

Quotations

"... but he never got the golden apple! He never left the cinder-heap on any of the three days."

1. Who said this? The brothers

2. Why did they say it? Because the King commanded that every man in the kingdom should come to the palace to see if he could show the golden apple.

Discussion Questions

1. Why do you think Cinderlad's brothers treat him so rudely?
2. Do you think it is destiny that Cinderlad is able to make it through the night and tame the horses? Or is he simply more courageous?

Enrichment

1. Cinderlad showed a lot of courage in the barn during the rumbling and the earthquake. Imagine that you are in the barn that night. What does it sound like? How do you feel? Would you run away like the other brothers, or would you stay there?

"… and he had really tried to cure himself of these defects, but by that time all his faults had become habits; and a bad habit is very hard to get rid of."

Reading Notes

resolution a firm decision to do or not do something

churlish being rude and difficult to deal with

menagerie a collection of wild animals kept in captivity for exhibition

Vocabulary

Definitions Bank

agreeing to do something

forced to leave a country as punishment

to prevent or stop someone from doing something

renewal; re-establishment

1. they may insult and **thwart** you as often as they please to prevent or stop someone from doing something
2. to try and frighten the shepherdess into **consenting** to marry him agreeing to do something
3. they now had a good opportunity of getting him **banished** for ever forced to leave a country as punishment
4. let us pity him and hope for his **restoration** renewal; re-establishment

Comprehension Questions

1. As an offer to the good King, what three things does the Fairy say she is willing to provide for his son, Prince Darling? Does the King ask for any of these three, or something else? She offers to make him the handsomest, the richest, or the most powerful. No, he does not ask for any of those; instead, he asks for his son to be the "best of princes"—that is, a good prince with excellent character.
2. What object does the Fairy give to Prince Darling as a young boy to help him be good? What does the object do? Do you think the object could be viewed as a **symbol** for something that we all have within us? What could it be? She gives him a gold ring that pricks him when he does a bad deed. Yes, the ring could very well be viewed as a symbol for the prick of our conscience.

3. Though Prince Darling does not want to admit any wrongdoing in beating his dog, the Fairy points out his three faults. What are they? First, he was mad because he could not have what he wanted; second, he thought all men and animals were made to do his pleasure; third, he was angry, and then cruel to a poor little animal who did not deserve to be ill-treated.

4. To help correct Prince Darling's thinking, and to instruct him, what does the Fairy say is the true advantage of possessing a great empire? She says that the advantage of possessing a great empire is not to be able to do the evil that one desires, but to do all the good that one possibly can.

5. What response does Celia give to Prince Darling when he says he wants to marry her? You may summarize what she says in your own words, or quote her directly using quotation marks. "No, my Prince," replied Celia. "I cannot help thinking you very handsome; but what good would riches be to me, and all the grand dresses and splendid carriages that you would give me, if the bad deeds which I should see you do every day made me hate and despise you?"

6. As a punishment for Prince Darling becoming wicked, what combination of animals does the Fairy turn him into? List each animal and the character trait of Prince Darling that it symbolizes.

lion – anger

wolf – greediness

snake – ungratefully turning upon one who was a second father

bull – churlishness

Quotations

"I would return good for evil," he said to himself, "and save the unhappy man's life."

1. Who said this? Prince Darling

2. Why is this quote important in the story? What crucial change takes place? It was Prince Darling's first act of love and kindness—and because of it, he was able to be changed from a monster to a dog. It begins his process of restoration.

Discussion Questions

1. Why do you think the Fairy is referred to as "Fairy Truth"?
2. Why is white the favorite color of Fairy Truth? What do you think white symbolizes?
3. Why do you think Celia is in the cave with an old hermit? What might he represent?

"Don't cry, Grettel, and sleep peacefully, for God is sure to help us."

Reading Notes

fret to worry or be anxious

conscience the inner sense of what is right or wrong in one's thoughts and actions

dearth an inadequate amount; a famine

malicious full of or showing malice, meanness, spitefulness

Vocabulary

Definitions Bank

a skillful action or movement

comforted; made to feel better

expressed disapproval or found fault with

luxurious; magnificent

1. this **maneuver** he repeated again and again a skillful action or movement
2. his conscience had **reproached** him for leaving his children behind expressed disapproval or found fault with
3. But he **consoled** his little sister, and said: "Don't cry, Grettel …" comforted; made to feel better
4. and laid a most **sumptuous** dinner before them luxurious; magnificent

Comprehension Questions

1. What is the stepmother's "solution" for the family's lack of food resources? How does the father feel about this plan? The stepmother suggests getting rid of Hansel and Grettel by leaving them in a thick wood so they will not be able to find their way home. The husband resists the idea—he feels he cannot find it in his heart to leave them in the woods.
2. How do Hansel and Grettel first find a way home from the woods? Hansel drops white pebbles along the path so they are able to follow the white pebbles out of the woods and back home.
3. What does it mean that the father's "conscience had reproached him for leaving his children behind"? Clearly the father has felt very guilty for leaving the children behind. His conscience has sounded loudly within, pronouncing judgment on his sin.

4. When do the children search for the breadcrumbs on the path? Do they find them? What happened to them? They search during the first night under the moonlight. No, the birds have eaten them all up.

5. Who leads the children to the sugar-and-cakes house? A little snow-white bird

6. How is Hansel able to trick the old woman into thinking that he is not gaining weight? He sticks a bone out of the cage, which she mistakes for a finger because her eyes are so dim.

7. How is Grettel able to trick the old woman? What is she able to do to her? She says she doesn't know how to creep into the oven to see if it's properly heated. This prompts the witch to show her how to do it—and then Grettel is able to shove her into the oven instead.

Quotations

"These are even better than pebbles," … and crammed his pockets full of them.

1. Who said this? Hansel

2. Why was this said? What are better than pebbles? They have just been freed from the old witch and have discovered boxes of pearls and precious stones.

Discussion Questions

1. Read aloud the short poem that Grettel calls out to the white duck. Have students memorize the poem.
2. What is your favorite part of this story? Why do you think it is so well known?
3. What do you think is the moral of this story?

Enrichment

1. Draw a picture of the old woman, a picture of the sugar-and-cakes house, or both.

Additional Space for Composition (Enrichment) Exercises

Additional Space for Composition (Enrichment) Exercises

DISCUSSION QUESTION ANSWERS

Prince Hyacinth and the Dear Little Princess

1. For most of the story, Prince Hyacinth thought his nose was the right size, and everyone else's nose was too small. Whom do you think is most to blame for Prince Hyacinth's faulty view of his nose?

   His mother the Queen, the teachers, and all of the adults surrounded him with this deception since he was a child.

2. Why do you suppose the Dear Little Princess was snatched away just as Prince Hyacinth was about to kiss her hand?

   The tale doesn't say, but it would probably have broken the curse and his nose would have become the right size.

Cinderella, or the Little Glass Slipper

1. Why do you think Cinderella's sisters treated her so terribly? Was it just because she was their stepsister, or something more?

   It should be interesting to explore with your children some of the internal motivations of the sisters. It was most likely jealousy and envy that motivated the sisters to mistreat Cinderella. But was it jealousy simply over her beauty … or something more, like her character?

2. Of what significance is the glass slipper? Could the glass slipper stand for something more important or greater?

   It should be fun to introduce your children to the idea of symbol. Keep it simple and just explain that some things have greater value than just the actual thing itself. For example, you can ask them about something from their childhood that is very special to them—like a blanket or stuffed animal. That object is much more than just cotton, right? In this story, the glass slipper is that which brings the truth to light! It reveals to the world who Cinderella really is.

Beauty and the Beast

1. What sets Beauty apart from her sisters?

   While she is more clever and prettier than her sisters, it is her character that really distinguishes her from her sisters. Beauty is simple, optimistic, and self-sacrificing. She is also grateful, kind, and non-materialistic.

2. What do you think is the most important idea in the story? Could Beauty's dream contain the most important idea?

The underlying message and truth is revealed to Beauty in her dream. Her dream contains the Central Idea of the fairy tale: "Do not let yourself be deceived by appearances."

Why the Sea is Salt

1. Did the poor brother *intentionally* not tell his rich brother how to stop the mill? Do you agree with the poor brother?

Yes, the story says, "and when hay-harvest came the rich brother got it, but the other had taken good care not to teach him how to stop it." Whether or not the students agree with the poor brother should yield a good discussion. In one sense, it may not have been right for the poor brother not to tell his rich brother. But in another sense, the rich brother seems to kind of deserve it!

Felicia and the Pot of Pinks

1. Does Felicia show compassion to Bruno? Do you think she should have?

Yes, a couple of times in the story she shows great compassion for Bruno. Answers should vary as far as what students think regarding whether she should have or not.

2. Felicia says, "Ah! madam … I am so happy that I should like everybody else to be happy too." Reflect on her words here. What virtues do they reveal?

Her words reveal the pure love and magnanimity that Felicia has in her heart. Regardless of how others treat her, she continues to love others and want the best for them. She wants others to share in her happiness.

Snow-White and Rose-Red

1. Why do you think the mother carries the red and white rose trees with her wherever she goes?

They are a symbol and reminder of her two beloved children, Snow-White and Rose-Red. Her children are off and married to the King and his brother, so she keeps the trees as a way to keep her children close to her heart.

2. What vice or character flaw does the dwarf have that makes him so rotten?

It seems to be his greed that causes him to be so nasty.

Toads and Diamonds

1. Do you think that what comes out of the daughters' mouths is symbolic?

   Yes, a very good assumption is that what comes out of the girls' mouths is symbolic of the value of kind and beautiful speech. As well, the items are symbolic of the girls' characters and hearts.

2. Discuss the **title** of the fairy tale. Does it capture what is most important in the tale?

   The title captures the primary symbols in the story. The toads represent the character of the eldest daughter, and the diamonds represent the character of the younger daughter.

The Princess on the Glass Hill

1. Why do you think Cinderlad's brothers treat him so rudely?

   The tale doesn't really say, but perhaps because they are jealous of him. He may have some qualities that they do not have—most likely he has good character while they have poor character.

2. Do you think it is destiny that Cinderlad is able to make it through the night and tame the horses? Or is he simply more courageous?

   There is no right answer here, but there is a slight feeling of fate, destiny—and certainly magic—in regard to Cinderlad being able to make it through the night in the barn and then find the horses. And finding the magical horses allows him to become the knight who can climb the glass hill and win the princess.

   Note: If you are going to discuss fate or destiny, you will probably have to first define and explain the concepts. You may or may not wish to do so.

Prince Darling

1. Why do you think the Fairy is referred to as "Fairy Truth"?

   This emphasizes her role as the bearer of truth in the story. She teaches the truth to Prince Darling and orchestrates the events so that the truth is brought to light.

2. Why is white the favorite color of Fairy Truth? What do you think white symbolizes?

   White is the color often associated with innocence, goodness, honesty, cleanliness, perfection, lightness, and understanding, et al.

3. Why do you think Celia is in the cave with an old hermit? What might he represent?

Celia is there perhaps because the story is about finding truth. The Fairy takes the form of an ascetic monk, a figure of spiritual and holy wisdom. Celia is perhaps seeking guidance and counsel from the monk. Everything culminates in this beautiful scene: The Fairy reveals herself, Prince Darling repents, they find love and marriage, Suliman is recognized for his faithfulness, and Celia and Prince Darling reign for many years in truth, goodness, and wisdom.

Hansel and Grettel

1. Read aloud the short poem that Grettel calls out to the white duck. Have students memorize the poem.

   Here are two children, mournful very,
   Seeing neither bridge nor ferry;
   Take us upon your white back,
   And row us over, quack, quack!

2. What is your favorite part of this story? Why do you think it is so well known?

   Answers will vary. The story has many resonances in other fairy tales from history around the world—essentially children having to outwit ogres and witches into whose hands they have unwittingly fallen.

3. What do you think is the moral of this story?

   Answers will vary. Here is one possibility:
   Always persevere. Hansel shows perseverance and ingenuity in the most difficult circumstances.

QUIZZES & TESTS

Quiz I

Prince Hyacinth and the Dear Little Princess / Cinderella

Name:______________________________________

Date:______________________ Score: _____/45 pts.

Vocabulary Matching: Write the letter of the vocabulary word on the line. (16 points)

_________ **1.** inconsolable

_________ **2.** comparison

_________ **3.** splendid

_________ **4.** dreadful

_________ **5.** odious

_________ **6.** awry

_________ **7.** civilities

_________ **8.** astonishment

a. wonderful; beautiful

b. twisted or turned; not straight

c. surprise; amazement

d. the act of comparing things to see how they are alike or different

e. unpleasant; hateful

f. not able to be comforted

g. good manners; politeness

h. terrible; horrible

Vocabulary Usage: Fill in the blank with the appropriate vocabulary word. (8 points)

Definitions Bank

civilities	splendid	dreadful	awry
astonishment	odious	inconsolable	comparison

1. The Queen was _____________ when she saw this great nose.

2. She went and sat down by her sisters, showing them a thousand _____________, giving them part of the oranges and citrons.

3. The prince made him a _____________ present as a reward for this good news.

4. Anyone but Cinderella would have dressed their heads _____________, but she was very good, and dressed them perfectly well.

Multiple Choice: Circle the best answer for each question. (10 points)

1. In "Prince Hyacinth," what must the King do to break the enchantment of the Princess whom he loves?
- **a.** jump three times around
- **b.** tread on her cat's tail
- **c.** tell her he loves her
- **d.** run a race

2. Why does the old woman, the Fairy, turn out to be so important to Prince Hyacinth?
   a. She is able bring the truth to him about his big nose.
   b. She continues to tell him that his nose is small.
   c. She offers him enchantment.
   d. She takes him on a wild journey.
3. What happens when Prince Hyacinth admits that his nose is too long?
   a. He is transported to the Dear Little Princess's castle.
   b. He gets to carry the Princess across a beautiful stream.
   c. The crystal prison breaks, he receives the lesson from the Fairy, and he marries the Princess.
   d. His nose remains long.
4. Where did Cinderella get her name?
   a. from her birth mother
   b. from her mother who made her do all kinds of difficult work
   c. from her father
   d. from being made to sit among the cinders and ashes
5. Choose the jobs that Cinderella's stepmother demanded she do.
   a. iron her sisters' linens
   b. scrub her sisters' bedrooms
   c. scour the dishes
   d. all of the above

Comprehension Short Answer: Answer each question or fill in the blanks. (6 points)

1. Write in your own words the moral or lesson that the old Fairy teaches Prince Hyacinth. ______________

   ____

2. How does Cinderella treat her sisters when it is revealed that the glass slipper fits her and she will become the princess? ____

Composition: Write a short paragraph answering the question. (5 points)

Do you think Cinderella should have forgiven her sisters? Why or why not? Be sure to write a topic sentence and some additional sentences that explain or support the topic sentence.

____

____

____

____

Quiz 2

Beauty and the Beast / Why the Sea is Salt

Name:________________________________

Date:____________________ Score: _____/45 pts.

Vocabulary Matching: Write the letter of the vocabulary word on the line. (16 points)

_________ **1.** haggled

_________ **2.** perilous

_________ **3.** obliged

_________ **4.** mischief

_________ **5.** desolate

_________ **6.** extravagance

_________ **7.** prudent

_________ **8.** fatigue

a. harm or trouble

b. dangerous; unsafe

c. extreme tiredness; exhaustion

d. required; compelled

e. bickered and argued over the price

f. wise; sensible

g. deserted; empty

h. wasteful and careless spending

Vocabulary Usage: Fill in the blank with the appropriate vocabulary word. (8 points)

Definitions Bank

perilous	obliged	prudent	mischief
haggled	desolate	extravagance	fatigue

1. All that he had left was a little house in a _____________ place.

2. But their father, who was more _____________, begged them to wait a little.

3. At first they would not hear of this, and _____________ and bargained with the man, but he stuck to what he said.

4. He had to sail far away over the _____________ sea for freights of salt.

Multiple Choice: Circle the best answer for each question. (10 points)

1. What two things does Beauty wish for from her father when he goes on a journey to retrieve his lost ship?

- **a.** jewelry and a rose
- **b.** her father's safety and a rose
- **c.** her father's safety and some gold from the ship
- **d.** one new dress and a necklace

2. What are some of the physical objects that Beauty sees in the castle to indicate that her dreams contain real and true messages?
   a. a table in which a picture of the Prince appears
   b. talking flowers
   c. a vase with a picture of her father
   d. the bracelet and portrait of the Prince who seems to wink at her

3. What is the most important idea in "Beauty and the Beast"?
   a. Trust your heart, not appearances.
   b. Love flowers, plants, and trees.
   c. Money and jewelry are the most important things in life.
   d. Work hard to earn a good living.

4. When the poor man gets home with the hand-mill, what is the first thing he asks it to grind?
   a. Christmas Eve supper
   b. more farm animals
   c. herrings and milk pottage
   d. fresh goat's milk

5. What is the rich brother's reaction to the poor brother's banquet feast that he throws for all his friends?
   a. He thinks it is funny.
   b. He is joyful and supportive.
   c. He is angry and envious.
   d. He doesn't care either way.

Comprehension Short Answer: Answer each question or fill in the blanks. (6 points)

1. How is Beauty different than her sisters? ______________________________

____

2. Why is the sea salty?______________________________

____

____

Composition: Write a short paragraph answering the question. (5 points)

If you had the magical hand-mill, what would you have it grind, and why?

____

____

____

____

Quiz 3

Felicia and the Pot of Pinks / Snow-White and Rose-Red

Name:______________________________

Date:____________________ Score: _____/45 pts.

Vocabulary Matching: Write the letter of the vocabulary word on the line. (16 points)

_________ **1.** bitterly

_________ **2.** brink

_________ **3.** murmured

_________ **4.** entreat

_________ **5.** diligent

_________ **6.** confiding

_________ **7.** precipice

_________ **8.** ingratitude

a. trusting; confidential

b. a cliff or steep ledge

c. extreme edge

d. being unthankful or ungrateful

e. painfully; emotionally

f. made a low, continuing sound

g. careful; hardworking

h. to beg; to ask for earnestly

Vocabulary Usage: Fill in the blank with the appropriate vocabulary word. (8 points)

Definitions Bank

murmured	bitterly	diligent	confiding
brink	entreat	ingratitude	precipice

1. When she reached it she sat down upon the _____________ to rest.
2. Don't keep me in suspense, I _____________ you; say that you will marry me.
3. And they were the sweetest and best children in the world, always _____________ and always cheerful.
4. They came up to them in the most _____________ manner.

Multiple Choice: Circle the best answer for each question. (10 points)

1. What magical thing did the Queen do to Felicia's pitcher and the water?
   - **a.** She turned the pitcher into a golden vessel and the water into nectar.
   - **b.** She turned the pitcher into a beautiful rose and the water into the smell of the forest.
   - **c.** She turned the pitcher into gold and diamonds and the water into the smell of roses.
   - **d.** She turned the pitcher into a small dog and the water into a cat.

2. What does Felicia offer the Queen instead of the pot of pinks?
   a. a jewel
   b. a necklace
   c. a ring
   d. a pot of reds
3. From whom does the bear want to protect his treasure?
   a. the wicked dwarfs
   b. the wild horses
   c. their stepmother
   d. the birds
4. What does the creature eagerly reach for each time after the children free him?
   a. all sorts of sumptuous things to eat
   b. ivory, gold, and platinum
   c. gold, pearls, precious stones
   d. goblets, swords, and shields
5. Who is the bear actually?
   a. an elf
   b. the King
   c. Snow-White and Rose-Red's brother
   d. the King's son

Comprehension Short Answer: Answer each question or fill in the blanks. (6 points)

1. What kind of person is Felicia? Discuss her character. Mention a specific example or two from the fairy tale in your answer. ____________________

____

____

____

____

2. At the end of "Felicia and the Pot of Pinks," whom does the Queen change to be gentle, polite, and grateful?

____

Composition: Write a short paragraph answering the question. (5 points)

In "Snow-White and Rose-Red," what do you think the red and white rose trees symbolize?

____

____

____

____

____

____

____

____

Quiz 4

Toads and Diamonds /
The Princess on the Glass Hill

Name:______________________________

Date:____________________ Score: _____/45 pts.

Vocabulary Matching: Write the letter of the vocabulary word on the line. (16 points)

_________	**1.** doted	**a.**	politeness; courtesy
_________	**2.** aversion	**b.**	showed excessive fondness or love
_________	**3.** civility	**c.**	sparkled; glittered; shined
_________	**4.** grumbling	**d.**	healthy growth
_________	**5.** vigor	**e.**	a strong dislike
_________	**6.** outlying	**f.**	distant; remote
_________	**7.** glistened	**g.**	complaining; muttering
_________	**8.** wager	**h.**	bet; gamble

Vocabulary Usage: Fill in the blank with the appropriate vocabulary word. (8 points)

Definitions Bank

doted	vigor	civility	glistened
aversion	outlying	grumbling	wager

1. At the same time she had a horrible ____________ for the youngest.

2. She wanted to see how far the ____________ and good manners of this pretty girl would go.

3. When the grass was in the height of its ____________, it was all eaten up.

4. But when evening drew near, Cinderlad rambled away to the ____________ field.

Multiple Choice: Circle the best answer for each question. (10 points)

1. How does the youngest daughter respond to the old woman who asks her for a drink?

- **a.** "Oh! I could never do that; I'm far too busy."
- **b.** "You don't say! I'd like to, but my mother is calling."
- **c.** "Oh! ay, with all my heart, Goody."
- **d.** "Am I come hither to serve you with water, pray?"

2. How does the Fairy appear to the eldest daughter, Fanny?
   a. as an old woman
   b. as a rabbit
   c. as her best friend
   d. as a glorious princess

3. At the end of "Toads and Diamonds," what happens to the youngest daughter?
   a. The King's son finds her and they get married.
   b. The Fairy turns her into a wealthy woman.
   c. She is discovered by the King and given the highest position in the castle.
   d. She remains poor and alone.

4. In "The Princess on the Glass Hill," when was the grass eaten up each year?
   a. May Day
   b. St. John's Eve
   c. St. Michaelmas
   d. Christmas Eve

5. What does Cinderlad hear when he stays in the barn? What does he see in the morning?
   a. a tornado and a tsunami; a large camel
   b. a rumbling sound and a waterfall; a large mule with a saddle
   c. a rumbling and earthquake; a big horse with armor for a knight
   d. beautiful but strange music; a large knight

Comprehension Short Answer: Answer each question or fill in the blanks. (6 points)

1. What comes out of each daughter's mouth? ______________________________

____

____

2. What kind of person is Cinderlad? Discuss his character. Mention a specific example or two from the fairy tale in your answer. ______________________________

____

____

Composition: Write a short paragraph answering the question. (5 points)

In "The Princess on the Glass Hill," describe what happens at the following point until the end of the story: *So Cinderlad was forced to go to the King's palace. "Hast thou the golden apple?" asked the King.*

____

____

____

____

____

____

____

Final Exam

Prince Darling /
Hansel and Grettel

Name:______________________________

Date:________________ Score: _____ /70 pts.

Vocabulary Matching: Write the letter of the vocabulary word on the line. (16 points)

_________ **1.** thwart
_________ **2.** consenting
_________ **3.** banished
_________ **4.** restoration
_________ **5.** maneuver
_________ **6.** reproached
_________ **7.** consoled
_________ **8.** sumptuous

a. renewal; re-establishment
b. a skillful action or movement
c. agreeing to do something
d. forced to leave a country as punishment
e. comforted; made to feel better
f. to prevent or stop someone from doing something
g. luxurious; magnificent
h. expressed disapproval or found fault with

Vocabulary Usage: Fill in the blank with the appropriate vocabulary word. (8 points)

Definitions Bank

sumptuous	banished	reproached	thwart
maneuver	consoled	restoration	consenting

1. You had better be accused of that by your subjects than that they should find out that they may insult and ____________ you as often as they please.
2. Try and frighten the shepherdess into ____________ to marry him.
3. They thought they now had an opportunity of getting him ____________ forever.
4. We may hate his faults, but let us pity him and hope for his ____________.
5. Hansel stood still and looked back at the house, and this ____________ he repeated again and again.
6. But the father rejoiced, for his conscience had ____________ him for leaving his children behind.
7. But he ____________ his little sister, and said "Don't cry, Grettel."
8. She took them both by the hand and let them into the house, and laid a most ____________ dinner before them—milk and sugared pancakes, with apples and nuts.

Multiple Choice: Circle the best answer for each question. (20 points)

1. As an offer to the good King, what things does the Fairy say she is willing to provide for his son, Prince Darling?
   - **a.** to be the most handsome
   - **b.** to be the richest
   - **c.** to be the most powerful
   - **d.** a and b
   - **e.** a, b, and c
   - **f.** none of the above
2. What does the King ask for his son?
   - **a.** to be the strongest son in the land
   - **b.** to be the best of princes (to be good)
   - **c.** to be famous and well known
   - **d.** to be sweet to his siblings
3. "I promised your father that I would be your friend, and to keep my word I have come to bring you a present. … Take great care of this ________, it is more precious than diamonds."
   - **a.** ruby
   - **b.** gold coin
   - **c.** rabbit
   - **d.** ring
4. Who says the quote in Question #3?
   - **a.** the King
   - **b.** Celia
   - **c.** the Fairy
   - **d.** Suliman
5. How does Prince Darling respond when he comes home from hunting and his little dog, Bibi, runs to meet him?
   - **a.** He kicks Bibi and says, "Get away!"
   - **b.** He picks up Bibi and strokes her lovingly.
   - **c.** He pets Bibi briefly and then lays out some food for her.
   - **d.** He is indifferent to Bibi, showing little emotion.
6. What object pricks Prince Darling, and what does the pricking symbolize?
   - **a.** gold coin; freedom
   - **b.** ring; conscience
   - **c.** furry cat; love
   - **d.** dog; friendship
   - **e.** glass egg; fate

7. "One day, he saw a young girl who was so very pretty that he made up his mind at once that he would marry her. Her name was ________, and she was as ________ as she was beautiful."
   a. Princess; forgiving
   b. Mary; simple
   c. Celia; good
   d. Elizabeth; fun

8. "No, my Prince," she replied. "I cannot help thinking you very handsome; but what good would riches be to me, and all the grand dresses and splendid carriages that you would give me, if the bad deeds which I should see you do every day made me hate and despise you?"
   a. Prince Darling understood how wise her speech was and repented of his ways.
   b. Prince Darling was angry and had her carried to his palace and made a prisoner.
   c. Prince Darling didn't think much about her words.
   d. Prince Darling accepted what she said and considered it for several days.

9. When he is given the throne, what does Suliman hope for that changes Prince Darling's perspective?
   a. He hopes for everyone to see Prince Darling's actions, and for him to be treated accordingly.
   b. He hopes that Prince Darling would be banished from the country and not allowed to return.
   c. He hopes that Prince Darling would be put in prison and punished for his wrongdoings.
   d. He hopes for everyone to pity Prince Darling and hope for his restoration.

10. What is the correct sequence of changes that Prince Darling undergoes?
   a. 4-animal monster; cat; eagle; Prince Darling
   b. 4-animal monster; panther; hummingbird; Prince Darling
   c. 4-animal monster; dog; dove; Prince Darling
   d. 4-animal monster; turtle; owl; Prince Darling

11. Why does Prince Darling change each time?
   a. He reproaches himself and repents.
   b. He tries to make himself change into a new creature.
   c. He learns what it takes to be a prince.
   d. He knows more than he used to know.

12. In "Hansel and Grettel," what is the stepmother's "solution" for the family's lack of food resources?
   a. Try to get Hansel and Grettel to go to work for the family.
   b. Leave Hansel and Grettel in a thick wood so they will not be able to find their way home.
   c. Start a family business to try to help pay for food.
   d. Trust in God to provide for their needs.

13. What does it mean that the father's "conscience had reproached him for leaving his children behind"?
   a. He knows it is a terrible thing to do, and he feels guilty.
   b. He thinks it is okay because the family is so poor.
   c. He loves his children tremendously, but loves their stepmother more.
   d. He hopes that the family will have enough to eat.

14. “Get up, you lie-abeds, we’re all going to the forest to fetch wood.” Who said this?
   a. Grettel
   b. Hansel
   c. Hansel and Grettel’s father
   d. Hansel and Grettel’s stepmother

15. “Be comforted, my dear little sister, and go to sleep: God will not desert us.” Who said this, and what does it reveal?
   a. Hansel; his faith and trust in God
   b. Grettel; her faith and trust in God
   c. their distant cousin; her desire for expensive jewelry and fine clothes
   d. their stepmother; her love for them

16. “What two things does Hansel leave on the path to try to find his way back home?
   a. breadcrumbs; little paper balls
   b. black pebbles; breadcrumbs
   c. breadcrumbs; marbles
   d. white pebbles; breadcrumbs

17. After the birds had eaten up their only chance to find their way back home, the children spend three days wandering, going deeper and deeper into the woods. Who comes to help them?
   a. a nearby woodcutter
   b. their father
   c. a little snow-white bird
   d. the old woman

18. When the children hear the shrill voice from inside the candy house, how do they answer, and what do they do?
   a. They answer back and keep eating.
   b. They run away quickly.
   c. They answer back, and then leave quickly.
   d. They go to the door to see who called to them.

19. What is it that the old woman has planned for the children?
   a. to keep them for company because she is lonely
   b. to cook them and eat them
   c. to play cards and games with them
   d. to allow them to leave whenever they would like

20. How does “Hansel and Grettel” end?
   a. They push the witch in the oven, gather pearls and precious stones, and reunite with their father.
   b. They escape by tricking the witch into going outside and looking for wood.
   c. They decide to stay and live with the witch.
   d. Hansel and Grettel’s stepmother rescues them.

Comprehension Short Answer: Answer each question or fill in the blanks. (12 points)

1. Explain how the Fairy analyzes Prince Darling's interaction with his dog. Summarize in detail her argument.

____

____

____

____

____

____

2. *"... and he had really tried to cure himself of these defects, but by that time all his faults had become habits; and a bad habit is very hard to get rid of."*

   Explain what important truth this quote reveals and why it is important for us to think about. __________

____

____

____

____

____

3. As a punishment for Prince Darling becoming wicked, what combination of animals does the Fairy turn him into? List each animal and the character trait of Prince Darling that it symbolizes.

__________ - ______________________________________

__________ - ______________________________________

__________ - ______________________________________

__________ - ______________________________________

4. Explain how Hansel is able to outsmart the witch when she tries to "fatten him up." ______________

____

____

____

____

____

Composition: Write a short paragraph answering the question. (14 points)

From any of the ten stories you have read, choose one that you think has the strongest moral message. Identify the story and its moral message, and then explain what things in the story reveal that message. You should write at least two paragraphs.

Quiz 1 Answer Key

Prince Hyacinth and the Dear Little Princess / Cinderella

Name:______________________________

Date:__________________ Score: _____/45 pts.

Vocabulary Matching: Write the letter of the vocabulary word on the line. (16 points)

f **1.** inconsolable
d **2.** comparison
a **3.** splendid
h **4.** dreadful
e **5.** odious
b **6.** awry
g **7.** civilities
c **8.** astonishment

a. wonderful; beautiful
b. twisted or turned; not straight
c. surprise; amazement
d. the act of comparing things to see how they are alike or different
e. unpleasant; hateful
f. not able to be comforted
g. good manners; politeness
h. terrible; horrible

Vocabulary Usage: Fill in the blank with the appropriate vocabulary word. (8 points)

Definitions Bank

civilities	splendid	dreadful	awry
astonishment	odious	inconsolable	comparison

1. The Queen was inconsolable when she saw this great nose.
2. She went and sat down by her sisters, showing them a thousand civilities, giving them part of the oranges and citrons.
3. The prince made him a splendid present as a reward for this good news.
4. Anyone but Cinderella would have dressed their heads awry, but she was very good, and dressed them perfectly well.

Multiple Choice: Circle the best answer for each question. (10 points)

1. In "Prince Hyacinth," what must the King do to break the enchantment of the Princess whom he loves?
   - **a.** jump three times around
   - **b.** tread on her cat's tail
   - **c.** tell her he loves her
   - **d.** run a race

2. Why does the old woman, the Fairy, turn out to be so important to Prince Hyacinth?
   a. She is able bring the truth to him about his big nose.
   b. She continues to tell him that his nose is small.
   c. She offers him enchantment.
   d. She takes him on a wild journey.
3. What happens when Prince Hyacinth admits that his nose is too long?
   a. He is transported to the Dear Little Princess's castle.
   b. He gets to carry the Princess across a beautiful stream.
   c. The crystal prison breaks, he receives the lesson from the Fairy, and he marries the Princess.
   d. His nose remains long.
4. Where did Cinderella get her name?
   a. from her birth mother
   b. from her mother who made her do all kinds of difficult work
   c. from her father
   d. from being made to sit among the cinders and ashes
5. Choose the jobs that Cinderella's stepmother demanded she do.
   a. iron her sisters' linens
   b. scrub her sisters' bedrooms
   c. scour the dishes
   d. all of the above

Comprehension Short Answer: Answer each question or fill in the blanks. (6 points)

1. Write in your own words the moral or lesson that the old Fairy teaches Prince Hyacinth. Answers will vary. Be honest with yourself; self-love is self-defeating.
2. How does Cinderella treat her sisters when it is revealed that the glass slipper fits her and she will become the princess? She forgives her sisters. She even offers them lodging in the palace.

Composition: Write a short paragraph answering the question. (5 points)

Do you think Cinderella should have forgiven her sisters? Why or why not? Be sure to write a topic sentence and some additional sentences that explain or support the topic sentence.

Answers will vary. Though her sisters do not deserve to be forgiven, it is right that Cinderella forgives them. Everyone needs forgiveness at some time, if not at many times. And it is in keeping with Cinderella's good character to forgive them.

Quiz 2 Answer Key

Beauty and the Beast / Why the Sea is Salt

Name:______________________

Date:______________ Score: _____/45 pts.

Vocabulary Matching: Write the letter of the vocabulary word on the line. (16 points)

e 1. haggled
b 2. perilous
d 3. obliged
a 4. mischief
g 5. desolate
h 6. extravagance
f 7. prudent
c 8. fatigue

a. harm or trouble
b. dangerous; unsafe
c. extreme tiredness; exhaustion
d. required; compelled
e. bickered and argued over the price
f. wise; sensible
g. deserted; empty
h. wasteful and careless spending

Vocabulary Usage: Fill in the blank with the appropriate vocabulary word. (8 points)

Definitions Bank

perilous	obliged	prudent	mischief
haggled	desolate	extravagance	fatigue

1. All that he had left was a little house in a desolate place.
2. But their father, who was more prudent, begged them to wait a little.
3. At first they would not hear of this, and haggled and bargained with the man, but he stuck to what he said.
4. He had to sail far away over the perilous sea for freights of salt.

Multiple Choice: Circle the best answer for each question. (10 points)

1. What two things does Beauty wish for from her father when he goes on a journey to retrieve his lost ship?
   a. jewelry and a rose
   b. her father's safety and a rose
   c. her father's safety and some gold from the ship
   d. one new dress and a necklace

2. What are some of the physical objects that Beauty sees in the castle to indicate that her dreams contain real and true messages?
   a. a table in which a picture of the Prince appears
   b. talking flowers
   c. a vase with a picture of her father
   d. the bracelet and portrait of the Prince who seems to wink at her
3. What is the most important idea in "Beauty and the Beast"?
   a. Trust your heart, not appearances.
   b. Love flowers, plants, and trees.
   c. Money and jewelry are the most important things in life.
   d. Work hard to earn a good living.
4. When the poor man gets home with the hand-mill, what is the first thing he asks it to grind?
   a. Christmas Eve supper
   b. more farm animals
   c. herrings and milk pottage
   d. fresh goat's milk
5. What is the rich brother's reaction to the poor brother's banquet feast that he throws for all his friends?
   a. He thinks it is funny.
   b. He is joyful and supportive.
   c. He is angry and envious.
   d. He doesn't care either way.

Comprehension Short Answer: Answer each question or fill in the blanks. (6 points)

1. How is Beauty different than her sisters? Beauty's character distinguishes her from her sisters. She is simple, optimistic, and self-sacrificing. She is also grateful, kind, and non-materialistic.

2. Why is the sea salty? A skipper had to sail to faraway seas to gather salt. He desired the mill so that it would grind salt and then he wouldn't have to sail so far for it. He couldn't get the mill to stop grinding. It continues to grind salt at the bottom of the sea today.

Composition: Write a short paragraph answering the question. (5 points)

If you had the magical hand-mill, what would you have it grind, and why?

Quiz 3 Answer Key

Felicia and the Pot of Pinks / Snow-White and Rose-Red

Name:____________________

Date:____________ Score: _____ /45 pts.

Vocabulary Matching: Write the letter of the vocabulary word on the line. (16 points)

e 1. bitterly

c 2. brink

f 3. murmured

h 4. entreat

g 5. diligent

a 6. confiding

b 7. precipice

d 8. ingratitude

a. trusting; confidential

b. a cliff or steep ledge

c. extreme edge

d. being unthankful or ungrateful

e. painfully; emotionally

f. made a low, continuing sound

g. careful; hardworking

h. to beg; to ask for earnestly

Vocabulary Usage: Fill in the blank with the appropriate vocabulary word. (8 points)

Definitions Bank

murmured	bitterly	diligent	confiding
brink	entreat	ingratitude	precipice

1. When she reached it she sat down upon the brink to rest.
2. Don't keep me in suspense, I entreat you; say that you will marry me.
3. And they were the sweetest and best children in the world, always diligent and always cheerful.
4. They came up to them in the most confiding manner.

Multiple Choice: Circle the best answer for each question. (10 points)

1. What magical thing did the Queen do to Felicia's pitcher and the water?
   a. She turned the pitcher into a golden vessel and the water into nectar.
   b. She turned the pitcher into a beautiful rose and the water into the smell of the forest.
   c. She turned the pitcher into gold and diamonds and the water into the smell of roses.
   d. She turned the pitcher into a small dog and the water into a cat.

2. What does Felicia offer the Queen instead of the pot of pinks?
   a. a jewel
   b. a necklace
   c. a ring
   d. a pot of reds
3. From whom does the bear want to protect his treasure?
   a. the wicked dwarfs
   b. the wild horses
   c. their stepmother
   d. the birds
4. What does the creature eagerly reach for each time after the children free him?
   a. all sorts of sumptuous things to eat
   b. ivory, gold, and platinum
   c. gold, pearls, precious stones
   d. goblets, swords, and shields
5. Who is the bear actually?
   a. an elf
   b. the King
   c. Snow-White and Rose-Red's brother
   d. the King's son

Comprehension Short Answer: Answer each question or fill in the blanks. (6 points)

1. What kind of person is Felicia? Discuss her character. Mention a specific example or two from the fairy tale in your answer. Felicia is magnanimous and loving. Regardless of how others treat her, she continues to love others and want the best for them. She says that she is so happy that she would like everyone else to be happy too.

2. At the end of "Felicia and the Pot of Pinks," whom does the Queen change to be gentle, polite, and grateful? Bruno

Composition: Write a short paragraph answering the question. (5 points)

In "Snow-White and Rose-Red," what do you think the red and white rose trees symbolize?
They are a symbol and reminder of the mother's two beloved children, Snow-White and Rose-Red. Her children are off and married to the King and his brother, so she keeps the trees as a way to keep her children close to her heart.

Quiz 4 Answer Key

Toads and Diamonds /
The Princess on the Glass Hill

Name:______________________________

Date:____________________ Score: _____/45 pts.

Vocabulary Matching: Write the letter of the vocabulary word on the line. (16 points)

b	**1.** doted	**a.**	politeness; courtesy
e	**2.** aversion	**b.**	showed excessive fondness or love
a	**3.** civility	**c.**	sparkled; glittered; shined
g	**4.** grumbling	**d.**	healthy growth
d	**5.** vigor	**e.**	a strong dislike
f	**6.** outlying	**f.**	distant; remote
c	**7.** glistened	**g.**	complaining; muttering
h	**8.** wager	**h.**	bet; gamble

Vocabulary Usage: Fill in the blank with the appropriate vocabulary word. (8 points)

Definitions Bank

doted	vigor	civility	glistened
aversion	outlying	grumbling	wager

1. At the same time she had a horrible ___aversion___ for the youngest.
2. She wanted to see how far the ___civility___ and good manners of this pretty girl would go.
3. When the grass was in the height of its ___vigor___, it was all eaten up.
4. But when evening drew near, Cinderlad rambled away to the ___outlying___ field.

Multiple Choice: Circle the <u>best</u> answer for each question. (10 points)

1. How does the youngest daughter respond to the old woman who asks her for a drink?
   - **a.** "Oh! I could never do that; I'm far too busy."
   - **b.** "You don't say! I'd like to, but my mother is calling."
   - **c.** "Oh! ay, with all my heart, Goody."
   - **d.** "Am I come hither to serve you with water, pray?"

2. How does the Fairy appear to the eldest daughter, Fanny?
   a. as an old woman
   b. as a rabbit
   c. as her best friend
   d. as a glorious princess

3. At the end of "Toads and Diamonds," what happens to the youngest daughter?
   a. The King's son finds her and they get married.
   b. The Fairy turns her into a wealthy woman.
   c. She is discovered by the King and given the highest position in the castle.
   d. She remains poor and alone.

4. In "The Princess on the Glass Hill," when was the grass eaten up each year?
   a. May Day
   b. St. John's Eve
   c. St. Michaelmas
   d. Christmas Eve

5. What does Cinderlad hear when he stays in the barn? What does he see in the morning?
   a. a tornado and a tsunami; a large camel
   b. a rumbling sound and a waterfall; a large mule with a saddle
   c. a rumbling and earthquake; a big horse with armor for a knight
   d. beautiful but strange music; a large knight

Comprehension Short Answer: Answer each question or fill in the blanks. (6 points)

1. What comes out of each daughter's mouth? The younger daughter: roses, pearls, and diamonds; the eldest daughter: vipers and toads

2. What kind of person is Cinderlad? Discuss his character. Mention a specific example or two from the fairy tale in your answer. Cinderlad is courageous and good. He is a man of strong faith. He seems to be chosen to pass the tests, tame the big horse, and win the Princess.

Composition: Write a short paragraph answering the question. (5 points)

In "The Princess on the Glass Hill," describe what happens at the following point until the end of the story: *So Cinderlad was forced to go to the King's palace. "Hast thou the golden apple?" asked the King.*

Cinderlad says yes and produces all three golden apples. He throws off his sooty clothes and appears before them in his bright golden armor. The King then says, "You shall have my daughter and half my kingdom; you have earned them both!" Then there is the wedding for Cinderlad and the King's daughter and everyone makes merry.

Final Exam Answer Key

Prince Darling /
Hansel and Grettel

Name:______________________________

Date:________________ Score: _____/70 pts.

Vocabulary Matching: Write the letter of the vocabulary word on the line. (16 points)

__f__ 1. thwart

__c__ 2. consenting

__d__ 3. banished

__a__ 4. restoration

__b__ 5. maneuver

__h__ 6. reproached

__e__ 7. consoled

__g__ 8. sumptuous

a. renewal; re-establishment

b. a skillful action or movement

c. agreeing to do something

d. forced to leave a country as punishment

e. comforted; made to feel better

f. to prevent or stop someone from doing something

g. luxurious; magnificent

h. expressed disapproval or found fault with

Vocabulary Usage: Fill in the blank with the appropriate vocabulary word. (8 points)

Definitions Bank

sumptuous	banished	reproached	thwart
maneuver	consoled	restoration	consenting

1. You had better be accused of that by your subjects than that they should find out that they may insult and __thwart__ you as often as they please.
2. Try and frighten the shepherdess into __consenting__ to marry him.
3. They thought they now had an opportunity of getting him __banished__ forever.
4. We may hate his faults, but let us pity him and hope for his __restoration__.
5. Hansel stood still and looked back at the house, and this __maneuver__ he repeated again and again.
6. But the father rejoiced, for his conscience had __reproached__ him for leaving his children behind.
7. But he __consoled__ his little sister, and said "Don't cry, Grettel."
8. She took them both by the hand and let them into the house, and laid a most __sumptuous__ dinner before them—milk and sugared pancakes, with apples and nuts.

Multiple Choice: Circle the best answer for each question. (20 points)

1. As an offer to the good King, what things does the Fairy say she is willing to provide for his son, Prince Darling?
   a. to be the most handsome
   b. to be the richest
   c. to be the most powerful
   d. a and b
   e. a, b, and c
   f. none of the above

2. What does the King ask for his son?
   a. to be the strongest son in the land
   b. to be the best of princes (to be good)
   c. to be famous and well known
   d. to be sweet to his siblings

3. "I promised your father that I would be your friend, and to keep my word I have come to bring you a present. ... Take great care of this _________, it is more precious than diamonds."
   a. ruby
   b. gold coin
   c. rabbit
   d. ring

4. Who says the quote in Question #3?
   a. the King
   b. Celia
   c. the Fairy
   d. Suliman

5. How does Prince Darling respond when he comes home from hunting and his little dog, Bibi, runs to meet him?
   a. He kicks Bibi and says, "Get away!"
   b. He picks up Bibi and strokes her lovingly.
   c. He pets Bibi briefly and then lays out some food for her.
   d. He is indifferent to Bibi, showing little emotion.

6. What object pricks Prince Darling, and what does the pricking symbolize?
   a. gold coin; freedom
   b. ring; conscience
   c. furry cat; love
   d. dog; friendship
   e. glass egg; fate

7. "One day, he saw a young girl who was so very pretty that he made up his mind at once that he would marry her. Her name was ________, and she was as ________ as she was beautiful."
   a. Princess; forgiving
   b. Mary; simple
   c. Celia; good
   d. Elizabeth; fun
8. "No, my Prince," she replied. "I cannot help thinking you very handsome; but what good would riches be to me, and all the grand dresses and splendid carriages that you would give me, if the bad deeds which I should see you do every day made me hate and despise you?"
   a. Prince Darling understood how wise her speech was and repented of his ways.
   b. Prince Darling was angry and had her carried to his palace and made a prisoner.
   c. Prince Darling didn't think much about her words.
   d. Prince Darling accepted what she said and considered it for several days.
9. When he is given the throne, what does Suliman hope for that changes Prince Darling's perspective?
   a. He hopes for everyone to see Prince Darling's actions, and for him to be treated accordingly.
   b. He hopes that Prince Darling would be banished from the country and not allowed to return.
   c. He hopes that Prince Darling would be put in prison and punished for his wrongdoings.
   d. He hopes for everyone to pity Prince Darling and hope for his restoration.
10. What is the correct sequence of changes that Prince Darling undergoes?
   a. 4-animal monster; cat; eagle; Prince Darling
   b. 4-animal monster; panther; hummingbird; Prince Darling
   c. 4-animal monster; dog; dove; Prince Darling
   d. 4-animal monster; turtle; owl; Prince Darling
11. Why does Prince Darling change each time?
   a. He reproaches himself and repents.
   b. He tries to make himself change into a new creature.
   c. He learns what it takes to be a prince.
   d. He knows more than he used to know.
12. In "Hansel and Grettel," what is the stepmother's "solution" for the family's lack of food resources?
   a. Try to get Hansel and Grettel to go to work for the family.
   b. Leave Hansel and Grettel in a thick wood so they will not be able to find their way home.
   c. Start a family business to try to help pay for food.
   d. Trust in God to provide for their needs.
13. What does it mean that the father's "conscience had reproached him for leaving his children behind"?
   a. He knows it is a terrible thing to do, and he feels guilty.
   b. He thinks it is okay because the family is so poor.
   c. He loves his children tremendously, but loves their stepmother more.
   d. He hopes that the family will have enough to eat.

14. "Get up, you lie-abeds, we're all going to the forest to fetch wood." Who said this?

- **a.** Grettel
- **b.** Hansel
- **c.** Hansel and Grettel's father
- **d.** Hansel and Grettel's stepmother

15. "Be comforted, my dear little sister, and go to sleep: God will not desert us." Who said this, and what does it reveal?

- **a.** Hansel; his faith and trust in God
- **b.** Grettel; her faith and trust in God
- **c.** their distant cousin; her desire for expensive jewelry and fine clothes
- **d.** their stepmother; her love for them

16. "What two things does Hansel leave on the path to try to find his way back home?

- **a.** breadcrumbs; little paper balls
- **b.** black pebbles; breadcrumbs
- **c.** breadcrumbs; marbles
- **d.** white pebbles; breadcrumbs

17. After the birds had eaten up their only chance to find their way back home, the children spend three days wandering, going deeper and deeper into the woods. Who comes to help them?

- **a.** a nearby woodcutter
- **b.** their father
- **c.** a little snow-white bird
- **d.** the old woman

18. When the children hear the shrill voice from inside the candy house, how do they answer, and what do they do?

- **a.** They answer back and keep eating.
- **b.** They run away quickly.
- **c.** They answer back, and then leave quickly.
- **d.** They go to the door to see who called to them.

19. What is it that the old woman has planned for the children?

- **a.** to keep them for company because she is lonely
- **b.** to cook them and eat them
- **c.** to play cards and games with them
- **d.** to allow them to leave whenever they would like

20. How does "Hansel and Grettel" end?

- **a.** They push the witch in the oven, gather pearls and precious stones, and reunite with their father.
- **b.** They escape by tricking the witch into going outside and looking for wood.
- **c.** They decide to stay and live with the witch.
- **d.** Hansel and Grettel's stepmother rescues them.

Comprehension Short Answer: Answer each question or fill in the blanks. (12 points)

1. Explain how the Fairy analyzes Prince Darling's interaction with his dog. Summarize in detail her argument.
   She says he has committed three faults. First, he was out of temper because he could not have what he wanted, and he thought all men and animals were only made to do his pleasure; second, he was really angry, which is very naughty indeed; third, he was cruel to a poor little animal who did not in the least deserve to be ill-treated.

2. *"… and he had really tried to cure himself of these defects, but by that time all his faults had become habits; and a bad habit is very hard to get rid of."*

   Explain what important truth this quote reveals and why it is important for us to think about.
   This reveals that when we allow our faults to become habits, they become very hard to get rid of. This is a true and unfortunate fact about the human condition. It reminds us how important it is to continually struggle against our faults.

3. As a punishment for Prince Darling becoming wicked, what combination of animals does the Fairy turn him into? List each animal and the character trait of Prince Darling that it symbolizes.
   lion - anger
   wolf - greediness
   snake - ungratefully turning upon one who was a second father
   bull - churlishness

4. Explain how Hansel is able to outsmart the witch when she tries to "fatten him up." When she attempted to feel his finger, he always put a bone out of the cage instead. Her eyes were so dim she couldn't see that it was a bone and therefore continued to feed him. This prolonged his life considerably.

Composition: Write a short paragraph answering the question. (14 points)

From any of the ten stories you have read, choose one that you think has the strongest moral message. Identify the story and its moral message, and then explain what things in the story reveal that message. You should write at least two paragraphs.